PREACHER

UNTIL THE END OF THE WORLD

Garth Ennis
Writer

Steve Dillon
Artist

Matt Hollingsworth
Pamela Rambo
Colorists

Clem Robins
Letterer

Glenn Fabry
Original covers

PREACHER created by
GARTH ENNIS and STEVE DILLON

PREACHER: UNTIL THE END OF THE WORLD

Published by DC Comics. Cover, introduction and compilation
copyright © 1997 DC Comics. All Rights Reserved.
Originally published in single magazine form as PREACHER 8-17.
Copyright © 1995, 1996 Garth Ennis and Steve Dillon.
All Rights Reserved. All characters, their distinctive likenesses and related indicia
featured in this publication are trademarks of Garth Ennis and Steve Dillon.
Vertigo is a trademark of DC Comics.
The stories, characters, and incidents featured in this publication are entirely fictional.
DC Comics, 1700 Broadway, New York, NY 10019
A division of Warner Bros. - An AOL Time Warner Company
Printed in Canada. Fourth Printing.
ISBN:1-56389-312-6

Cover painting by Glenn Fabry.
Publication design by Jim Chadwick/Suddenly Chadwick!

INTRODUCTION
by Kevin Smith

This is sort of a story about how you can't please everybody (or in some cases, anybody).

The last time I said something nice about PREACHER, the good folks who compile the trade paperbacks at DC pulled a quote from my gushing praise of the parties involved in bringing this fierce new book to life, and they printed it on the cover – along the top and above the title.

That *really* put a smile on my face. Not only was my name finally on a comic book (sort of) – but it was on a compilation of a fantastic comic book that I wish anybody (or in some cases, everybody) would give a try. I was honored that any sort of connection would forever be made between this brave, original entry into the art form called comics, and myself.

For the record, the pull quote was "More fun than going to the movies!," complete with my name and then-filmography printed underneath.

Then it dawned on me: I was suddenly a very easy target.

And – as with all easy targets – some zero took perhaps the easiest shot in the world at me.

Hiding within a then-current issue of The Comics Journal, at the bottom of the 'Viva la Comics!' section, was my quote and credits – over which was the oh-so-damn-witty headline "Well, maybe one of *yours* ..."

Everyone's a comedian...

It was my fault, however – if you hang your balls out like that, there's always at least one person who wants to introduce them to a swift kick (a routine occurrence in my line of work, actually).

So you can imagine my trepidation when Garth asked me to write an intro for this collection...

...Actually, you can't.

Because there was none.

See, I'd risk getting kicked in the balls again to gush over PREACHER. And why? Because Garth hangs a great deal more than his balls out with every issue, and risks far more than just a kick by fashioning an ongoing tale that's packed wall-to-wall with thought-provoking commentary on religion and spirituality (fave-rave topics of mine).

We're instructed from an early age that discussion of religion is a social faux pas — that to talk about God is to possibly offend someone. Garth must have been absent when they taught that lesson, or perhaps chose to ignore it. And thank God he did — because in the pages of PREACHER, Mister Ennis talks about faith, spirituality, religion, and hypocrisy in a fashion that any publisher responsible for putting out the monthly antics of flying, invulnerable and magic-ring-bearing men would have to be near-crazy (or perhaps just plain smart) to mass-market. Usually such work is cited as "too controversial."

"Controversial," as we all know, is often a euphemism for "interesting and intelligent." Although the pages of PREACHER are filled with avant garde takes on the nature of God and the questionable manner in which religion is followed by the masses without thought (not to mention renderings of brutal bloodletting and graphic, often disturbingly funny violence), this is not a book full of sensationalistic crap writing or drawing. To me, sensationalistic crap writing is lopping off the hand of a time-honored character to give him a "new direction," and sensationalistic crap drawing is page after page of uber-nimrods penned with little regard for proper proportions, set against background-deficient splash pages.

Garth and Steve fall prey to none of that — they tell straightforward stories with the enviable skill often found only possessed by those who've spent years honing their craft. And while both have achieved respectability and kudos prior to their current endeavor (see Garth and Steve's run on HELLBLAZER, not to mention Garth's Fleetway-published *True Faith*), it is on PREACHER that both have hit their to-date creative zenith — a synergism that has produced the most scintillating and — I'll say it — *brilliant* piece of comics literature to come down the pike since DC landed Moore, Gaiman, and Morrison (why are non-Americans so much better at this than most?).

In the Angelville saga, Garth has basically told us something that we've known all along - family can be a scary thing. Whether it's the gotta-have-a-member-of-the-cloth-in-the-family-demanding Gran'ma, the chicken-fucking T.C., or the ready-to-make-a-man-out-of-ya Jody, the reader has to see some uncomfortable similarities (albeit distant ones, I'd hope) to his or her own dysfunctional family tree.

Not that it's all evil in this tale of woe. Garth gives us two powerful tastes of star-cros't love in the poignant flashbacks to both the gob-in-the-face introduction of Jesse's parents, and the knew-it-when-I-

laid-eyes-on-him/her romance of Jesse and Tulip. And from the more
orally amorous interpretation of "star-gazing," to Jesse's declaration of
"Until the end of the world," Garth and Steve flesh out a relationship both
credible and familiar.

But at the same time, if one looks closely, the true malevolent
fuck of the story isn't Jody - although his cold proclamation of "You come
with us quiet and make no fuss, or I'll shoot her through the fuckin' head,"
would certainly make him a candidate for the title. No - the real black
soul is the Ennis/Dillon team who actually make good on Jody's threat -
albeit temporarily - with the last panel of "How I Learned to Love the Lord"
(I can't remember another piece of graphic art leaving me as speechless or
as manically anxious to get my hands on the next installment).

The "Hunters" storyline introduces yet another wicked pair of
Ennis and Dillon creations. In The Grail, we find a bunch who know
something about Christ himself that would send Christians the world over
first to the nearest bar, and subsequently to collect every donated cent
back from Holy Mother Church. And in Jesus de Sade, we meet the ultimate
in debauchery, whose casual aside of "Ah, Demi - I do hope I'll have the
pleasure of urinating into your cleavage later?" and fistful of
chocolate (...or is it?) make for the most delightfully decadent and evil
arsehole this side of the Moore-scripted Anton Arcane.

Throw in an Irish vampire, a couple of titty-shots, some marathon,
catch-up in-and-out sessions, and the best dialogue being written in comics
today, and you've got some damned exquisite and thought-provoking
entertainment. And for those who missed it the first time, I'll say it
again - this book *is* more fun than going to the movies...

...even mine.

Garth and Steve have accomplished nothing short of a miracle in
PREACHER - producing a hot new title that actually *surpasses* its hype.
They are to be congratulated, envied, marveled at, and well paid.

And if this book offends the delicate sensibilities of some people due
to their religious convictions - well, that saddens me. Because, as a man
who has an unflappable, fervent, and devout faith in God, let me assure
those who find this book spiritually questionable that I know - in my heart
and soul - the Lord to be mighty, just, loving, and righteous...

...and a huge fan of PREACHER.

Kevin Smith

Kevin Smith has made three movies to date. The first one was set in a convenience store and
received huge praise and awards at the Sundance and Cannes Film Festivals (Clerks). The
second was set in an indoor shopping center, got trashed by critics and tanked at the box
office... but was still kind of funny (Mallrats). The third one - set in the comic-book
industry - isn't out yet, though people who've seen it seem to like it (Chasing Amy).

His next assignment is putting words in the mouth of Clark Kent and his Kryptonian alter ego
in the new Superman movie from Warner Bros.

THE FIRST HIT WAS A GUY, OH, I CAN'T REMEMBER THE REASON FOR IT. SOME CRAP TO DO WITH TURF.

ALL HIS BOYS ARE PACKIN', SO YOU PUT 'EM ALL DOWN BEFORE THEY GET IN THE CAR. THEN POP TWO IN HIS HEAD AND MOVE YOUR ASS.

GOT IT?

I GUESS THE OLD TULIP HADN'T GONE TOO FAR AFTER ALL. I MEAN, ONCE I ACTUALLY SAW HIM, I *KNEW* I COULD NEVER HAVE DONE IT...

I SCREWED UP SPECTACULARLY. IT WAS WHILE I WAS RUNNING AWAY THAT I RAN INTO YOU-KNOW-WHO.

THAT MACAVOY I HEARD YOU WITH ON THE PHONE?

YEAH. HE STILL WANTS HIS MONEY BACK.

WELL, THE HELL WITH HIM.

WE'LL GO SEE THE SON OF A BITCH FIRST THING WE HIT TOWN. I'M GONNA TELL HIM TO STICK HIS MONEY UP HIS ASS.

GIVES ME ANY SHIT, HE'LL FIND HIMSELF DOIN' IT LITERALLY: *EVERY FUCKIN' CENT.*

THANKS.

BUT THEN IT'S YOUR TURN IN THE CONFESSIONAL, OKAY?

OKAY.

THIS IS REALLY GOOD OF YOU, YOU KNOW. IT MUST BE A SHOCK TO KNOW I NEARLY KILLED SOMEONE.

YEAH, BUT LIKE YOU SAID, I AIN'T EXACTLY A REGULAR GUY EITHER. AN' AS FOR CASS...

GONNA HAVE A GODDAMN FREAK SHOW GOIN', WE AIN'T TOO CAREFUL.

BIG BAD MAC'S

HE'S NOT WHAT YOU'D EXPECT, IS HE? NO CAPE, NO BATS, NO GARLIC --I DON'T EVEN THINK HE'S GOT FANGS...

AND ISN'T HE MEANT TO HAVE A CASTLE IN EUROPE OR SOMEWHERE, INSTEAD OF A PICKUP TRUCK IN DALLAS?

SAID HE ORIGINALLY CAME DOWN HERE TO OPEN A BAR.

WANTED TO CALL IT "THE GRASSY KNOLL."

HOLY FUCKIN' DOGSHIT, THAT WHO I THINK IT IS?

WE'RE CLOSED. MR. MACAVOY AIN'T SEEIN' NO ONE.

HE'LL SEE ME.

MISS O'HARE...!

16

HELL YOU BRING THE GODDAMN REVER'ND FOR? YOU JOINED THE FUCKIN' MORMONS OR SOMETHIN'?

WOULD YOU JUST LISTEN FOR A MINUTE? PLEASE?

I'M SORRY I SCREWED UP THE JOB AND I'M SORRY I DON'T HAVE YOUR MONEY YET. BUT IF YOU CAN GIVE ME A LITTLE MORE TIME--

FUCK I WANNA DO THAT FOR?

'CAUSE OTHERWISE YOU'LL BE IN A WORLD OF HURT FOR THE REST'VE YOUR MISERABLE FUCKIN' LIFE.

AN' HERE I AM THINKIN' I GOT MY THREE BOYS TO JUST YOU AN' THE LADY, REVER'ND. COMES AS A SHOCK YOU HAD US OUTGUNNED ALL ALONG.

'KAY, TIE HER UP. TAKE THIS COCKSUCKER DOWNSTAIRS AN' BREAK HIS GODDAMN NECK.

WE'RE CLOSED. MR. MACAVOY AIN'T SEEIN' NO ONE.

YOU STILL HERE?

JESUS CHRIST...

WANNA TRY THAT AGAIN, BOYZ?

YOU--

GODDAMN YOU, JODY. YOU DROP THAT FUCKIN' GUN.

'KAY, NOW WE GOT THAT SETTLED.

GONNA TAKE US A WALK OUTSIDE. T.C.'S GOT THE VAN READY. ANY BULLSHIT, I SHOOT YOU IN THE LEGS AN' HER IN THE FACE. MAYBE LET T.C. PUT THE DICK TO HER FIRST, SO JUST BEHAVE YOUR FUCKIN' SELF.

LET'S GO.

DO LIKE HE SAYS.

er...

YOU CAN GO TAKE A BIG OL' SUCK ON THE DEVIL'S PECKER, FAT BOY.

NEARLY THERE.

THE RATE WE'VE BEEN GOING, WE MUST BE IN LOUISIANA BY NOW...

uh-huh.

RIGHT ON THE STATE LINE.

JESSE, *PLEASE,* WHAT'S ALL THIS ABOUT--

TOLD YOU, HONEY. SHUT UP. FIND OUT SOON ENOUGH.

JODY, LOOK...

YOU GOT ME, OKAY? I'M THE ONE YOU NEED, NOT HER. LET HER GO.

I'M FUCKIN' BEGGIN' YOU: *PLEASE.*

uh-uh. YOU WENT MISSIN', WE WERE TOLD TO BRING YOU BACK AN' ANYONE ALONG WITH YOU. YOU CARIN' 'BOUT HER JUST MAKES IT MORE DEFINITE SHE COMES TOO.

SHOULDA DONE THE RIGHT THING, BOY. THINGS GOT ALL FUCKED UP IN ANNVILLE, YOU SHOULDA COME ON HOME.

YOU SHOULDA TRUSTED YOUR *GRAN'MA,* BOY.

ANKLES IN BEHIND THEM CHAIRLEGS. DON'T WANT 'EM MOVIN' 'ROUND THE ROOM.

TIGHT, NOW.

TULIP, LISTEN TO ME NOW: I KNOW YOU GOT ABOUT A HUNDRED QUESTIONS YOU WANNA ASK, BUT YOU GOTTA STAY QUIET.

NO MATTER WHAT HAPPENS, NO MATTER WHAT YOU SEE HERE: ONLY CHANCE YOU GOT IS NOT TO SAY A GODDAMN WORD.

BUT... BUT WHAT ABOUT YOU...?

FOR CHRIST'S SAKE--!

WANNA SMOKE, BOYZ?

FUCK YOUR- SELF.

CHANGE YOUR MIND, YOU LEMME KNOW.

SONUVABITCH--!

SHE'S HERE, JODY.

GOOD EVENING, BOYS...

25

MOTHER-FUCKER!!

I'M TELLIN' YOU, JODY, I'M TELLIN' YOU RIGHT FUCKIN' NOW, **I'M GONNA KILL YOU!**

I'M GONNA CHOKE THE FUCKIN' BLACK SOUL FROM YOUR WORTH-LESS CORPSE AN' I'M GONNA DO IT WITH MY OWN TWO HANDS, I SWEAR TO GOD!

I SWEAR TO FUCKIN' GOD, **YOU ARE DEAD!**

TRIED IT BEFORE, BOY.

'MEMBER?

MY, BUT DON'T YOU HAVE A HEAD OF STEAM WORKED UP, JESSE?

YOU'VE STILL GOT PLENTY OF THAT TEXAS WHITE TRASH FATHER OF YOURS IN YOU, HAVEN'T YOU? THAT WORTH-LESS WASTE OF LIFE WHO LEFT YOU NOTHING BUT HIS NAME...

THAT'S ALL I'LL EVER NEED.

I HEARD STUFF FROM GUYS ON THEIR SECOND TOURS, YOU KNOW? HOW THERE WASN'T NO HERO'S WELCOME WAITIN' BACK HOME, LIKE OUR DADDIES GOT IN WORLD WAR TWO...

BUT GETTIN' BACK WAS THE GOLD AT THE END OF THE RAINBOW FOR ME. I NEVER BELIEVED WHAT I HEARD --JUST KEPT MY HEAD DOWN, GOT SHORT, FOCUSED ON THE BIG GOLDEN HOMECOMING.

I GUESS I SHOULDN'T BE SO GODDAMN ARROGANT.

I NEVER KILLED NO BABIES, BUT I AIN'T DENYIN' I SAW AN' DID SOME POINTLESS, FUCKED-UP THINGS OVER THERE.

AN' IF I WAS BEIN' HONEST, I'D HAVE TO SAY IT WAS 'CAUSE SOMEONE TOLD ME IT WAS THE RIGHT THING TO DO...

GET ME?

OH YEAH.

SO...JOHN CUSTER...

SO, CHRISTINA L'ANGELLE... AN' DAMNED IF THAT AIN'T THE PRETTIEST NAME I EVER HEARD...

YOU MIGHT NOT THINK SO, IF YOU KNEW WHAT WENT ALONG WITH IT.

BUT: WHAT DO YOU SAY WE BOTH QUIT LISTENING TO WHAT OTHER PEOPLE SAY WE OUGHT TO DO...

AN' START FIGURIN' IT OUT FOR OURSELVES...?

MM-HM.

THESE TWO AN' THEIR FUCKIN' STRAIGHT-FROM HELL KIN, THEY BEEN SERVIN' MY GRAN'MA'S FAMILY SINCE TIME MEANT SHIT. T.C.'S JUST A SNEAKY FUCK LIKES TO STICK HIS DICK IN ANY CRITTER WITH A PULSE--

BUT JODY...

WAY I FIGURE IT, HE MAYBE GOT FUCKED *BAD* WHEN HE WAS LITTLE. LIKE IN THE WOMB.

'CAUSE JODY IS NOW THE *LEADING EXPERT* ON FUCKING PEOPLE OVER BEFORE THEY CAN FUCK HIM. HE'S STRONG AS SHIT, BORN MEAN, GOT A REAL *INTELLIGENCE* GLEAMIN' IN THEM EYES--

LAST LESSON HE HAD TO LEARN, MY DAD TAUGHT HIM TWENTY YEARS AGO.

YOU FUCKED UP, GIRL. YOU BETTER COME ALONG WITH US NOW, 'FORE YOU MAKE IT ANY WORSE.

JOHN, NO! I KNOW THEM! THEY'RE KILLERS!

THEY'RE TRASH WITH GUNS, IS ALL THEY ARE.

YOU HOLD THIS FOR ME, T.C.?

41

DAD!

SAY YOUR PRAYERS COCK-SUCKER--

JOHN!

...OH FUCK, WAIT A MINUTE.

"DAD"?

JODY, I THINK WE GOT US A PROBLEM...

NO SHIT?

SO THEY PACKED US IN A VAN AND BROUGHT US BACK HERE TO ANGELVILLE.

YOU MET GRAN'MA ALREADY, TOO. FIGURE SHE MUST'VE BEEN ABOUT EIGHTY THEN-- HELL, YOU AIN'T GONNA BELIEVE THIS, BUT THE OLD BITCH HAD MY MOM WHEN SHE WAS SIXTY.

I DUNNO HOW THE FUCK IT'S POSSIBLE--

UNLESS THE L'ANGELLES GOT MORE'N JUST BLOOD IN THEIR VEINS.

DEVIL'S OWN PISS, IS WHAT I FIGURE.

THEY'RE A FRENCH PURITAN FAMILY, SETTLED HERE AROUND THE TIME OF NAPOLEON. CONVERTED THE LOCAL INDIANS TO CORPSES--CHEAPER'N CHRISTIANITY --AN' SET ABOUT SPREADIN' THE WORD TO ANY SETTLERS DUMB ENOUGH TO SHOW UP.

ALL THE MEN WERE PREACHERS 'CEPT IN TIME OF WAR. THE WOMEN WERE MEANT FOR NOTHIN' MORE'N BREEDIN' THE NEXT GENERATION, WHICH THEY TOOK TO REAL WELL. FAMILY GOES *WAY BACK*. BLOOD IS *EVERYTHING*.

GRAN'MA'S KEEPIN' UP THE TRADITION WITH A VENGEANCE, BELIEVE ME. COULDN'T FIND ANY- ONE TO MARRY HER TILL SHE WAS OVER FIFTY--

PROBABLY 'CAUSE SHE WAS BORN WITH A FACE LIKE *DRIED-UP SHIT*.

AN' A SOUL TO MATCH.

JOHN CUSTER, YOU WILL MARRY MY DAUGHTER.

YOU WILL BOTH LIVE *HERE* WITH YOUR SON JESSE, AS A PROPER FAMILY IN THE EYES OF THE LORD. YOU WILL CARE FOR THEM AS A HUSBAND AND FATHER. YOU WILL GROOM YOUR SON FOR HIS DESTINY AS A MAN OF GOD. YOU WILL *NEVER* LEAVE THIS PLACE.

IF A DAY COMES ON WHICH YOU ARE FOOLISH ENOUGH TO *TRY:*

YOU WILL DIE.

AN' COME THAT DAY, BOY:

YOU'RE MINE.

SO MARRIED WAS WHAT THEY GOT.

I DON'T REMEMBER MUCH ABOUT BEIN' FOUR, EXCEPT WE STOPPED GOIN' TO THE MOVIES AN' I COULDN'T STAY UP LATE ANYMORE...

BUT DAD WASN'T SITTIN' STILL. HE WAS SMART ENOUGH TO HOLD OFF FOR THE RIGHT TIME TO MAKE A BREAK--LIKE MOM HAD FIVE YEARS PREVIOUS, AN' I WOULD A DOZEN YEARS LATER.

NO WAY WAS HE GONNA LET HIS WIFE AN' KID LIVE AT THE MERCY OF TRASH, NOT KNOWING WHAT KINDA SHIT WAS PLANNED FOR US:

DAMNED IF HE WAS.

SO ONE DAY, NOT LONG AFTER I TURNED FIVE, DAD CAME AN' TOLD ME WE WERE LEAVIN'.

I NEED YOU TO BE BRAVE FOR ME, SON.

AN' I NEED YOU TO KNOW SOME THINGS, IN CASE WE... WE DON'T GET A CHANCE TO TALK ABOUT 'EM LATER.

I LOVE YOU, JESSE. YOU'RE MY OWN SON AN' I'M PROUD OF YOU, AN' YOU BROUGHT YOUR MOM AN' ME MORE HAPPINESS THAN I EVER KNEW THERE WAS. YOU BE GOOD TO HER, AN' LOOK AFTER HER.

AN' YOU BE A GOOD GUY, JESSE. YOU GOTTA BE LIKE *JOHN WAYNE*: YOU DON'T TAKE NO SHIT OFF FOOLS, AN' YOU JUDGE A PERSON BY WHAT'S IN 'EM, NOT HOW THEY LOOK.

AN' YOU DO THE *RIGHT* THING.

YOU *GOTTA* BE ONE OF THE GOOD GUYS, SON:

'CAUSE THERE'S WAY TOO MANY OF THE BAD.

AN' THEY CAUGHT US BEFORE WE GOT TWO MILES, AN' THEY SHOT MY DADDY IN THE HEAD.

THAT WAS THE LAST TIME I EVER CRIED.

STOOD THERE AN' BAWLED MY HEART OUT, SCREAMED AN' SCREAMED, 'TIL JODY TURNED TO ME AN' SAID

FUCKIN' LITTLE CRYBABY.

AN' I WAS ONLY FIVE BUT SUDDENLY I KNEW WHAT DAD HAD MEANT, ABOUT TOO MANY OF THE BAD GUYS...AN' I KNEW JOHN WAYNE NEVER CRIED...

SO NEITHER DID I.

AFTER THAT, MOM WAS ABOUT CUT IN TWO AS A PERSON. SHE'D RUN AWAY FROM ANGELVILLE AN' HER MOTHER, AN' NOW THEY'D REACHED OUT AN' BROUGHT HER BACK, AN' TAKEN EVERYTHING SHE'D EVER CARED FOR FROM HER.

GRAN'MA KNEW WHO HELD THE ACES. SHE COULD GIVE US BOTH A LITTLE, JUST TO TAKE A LOT--WE WEREN'T GOIN' ANYWHERE, BUT KEEPIN' US SWEET WOULD PAY OFF FOR HER...

SO I GUESS ME AN' A NORMAL CHILDHOOD KIND OF PASSED LIKE SHIPS IN THE NIGHT. ONLY NODS I GOT TO IT WERE TV...

MY LITTLE DOG DUKE...

AND MY BEST FRIEND BILLY-BOB.

BILLY-BOB'S FOLKS LIVED WAY OUT IN THE BAYOU. I FIGURE HE LOOKED THE WAY HE DID 'CAUSE SOMEONE DUMPED CHEMICALS IN THE SWAMP, WAY IT HAPPENED IN THE CARTOONS.

TURNED OUT IT WASN'T THAT AT ALL...

YOU EVER WONDER WHO YOU'RE GONNA GROW UP TO MARRY, BILLY-BOB?

NOPE.

GONNA MARRY MY SISTER LORIE.

WAY IT'S ALWAYS WORKED IN MY FAMILY, OLDEST BOY MARRIES THE OLDEST GIRL. MY MOM AN' DAD ARE BROTHER AN' SISTER, SEE?

DAD SAYS IT'S GOOD 'CAUSE IT LETS US KEEP OUR BLOODLINE...

I DUNNO WHAT THAT IS, BUT I GUESS IT'S GOOD TO KEEP ONE.

I...I AIN'T GOT NO SISTER, BILLY-BOB.

WELL, YOU CAN STILL GET MARRIED--

WHOA! JESSE! LOOK!

PULL 'IM IN, JESSE! BIG OL' CHANNEL CAT! YEEE-HA!

WARF!

HELL, WE WERE SEVEN. WE OWNED THE WORLD.

...WHY YOU LOOKIN' AT ME LIKE THAT?

NO REASON.

SO EVEN THOUGH I WAS SCARED OF A GUY WHO SAW EVERYTHING I DID, AND I COULDN'T GET IT STRAIGHT HOW HE LIVED IN MY HEART, I PRETTY SOON REALIZED THE RIGHT ANSWER WAS

YES.

IT WAS NICE TO HAVE A FRIEND LIKE GOD.

I WAS SEVEN.

SO IT WENT. I HAD TO LEARN A PAGE OF THE BIBLE EVERY DAY, AN' MOM TAUGHT ME OTHER STUFF: ENGLISH, MATH, LITTLE BIT OF HISTORY. CLEVER LADY, MY MOM.

BUT LIKE I TOLD YOU, HER HEART LEFT HER WHEN DAD GOT SHOT. AN' EVEN THOUGH SHE LOVED ME, AN' SHE WANTED TO GET ME OUT'VE ANGELVILLE MORE'N *ANYTHING*--

YOU COULD SEE, MAYBE ONCE A DAY AT LEAST, ALL SHE WANTED WAS TO GO ON AN' BE WITH DAD.

I NEVER THOUGHT BAD OF HER FOR IT.

LAST DAY I SAW HER, I WAS ELEVEN. ME AN' BILLY-BOB WERE TOO BUSY WATCHIN' WILE E. COYOTE TO PLAY WITH DUKE...

WHAT YOU RECKON HE'S GONNA DO WITH THE ROADRUNNER, HE EVER CATCHES IT?

T.C. SAYS HE'S GONNA STICK HIS PECKER IN IT.

HUH?

SAYS THAT'S WHAT HE'D DO.

WARF.

GRAN'MA HAS IT.

I'M ... SORRY...

WOMEN'RE JUST FOR BREEDIN' THE NEXT GENERATION. BLOOD IS EVERYTHING. ALL THE DECISION WAS TO GRAN'MA, WAS MATH.

GET OFF ME ! GET YOUR FUCKING HANDS OFF ME ! JESSEEEE!!

JESSSEEEEE!

ALL THIS OVER A GODDAMN DOG...

YOU GET ALONG HOME, YOU ONE-EYED FUCK.

DO YOU SEE WHAT YOU'VE DONE?

AN' THEY DRAGGED HER AWAY IN FRONT OF MY EYES.

BETWEEN THE STINK OF MY SHIT AN' PUKE AN' PISS AN' THE NOISE FROM WHAT WAS CRAWLIN' AROUND OUTSIDE, MY WEEK IN THE COFFIN KIND OF SUCKED.

HOW I LEARNED TO LOVE THE LORD

YOU COULD BREATHE THROUGH THE TUBE OKAY, BUT THAT WAS IT FOR THE GOOD NEWS. YOU COULDN'T FIGURE TIME, YOU COULDN'T SEE A GODDAMN THING, YOU *STARVED*...

JESSE, YOU WERE A LITTLE KID! HOW IN CHRIST'S NAME DID YOU *STAND* IT?

...

WISH I KNEW.

HOW YOU DOIN', LITTLE JESSE?

AAAHH!

OPEN THEM EYES.

NO! LEMME GO! HURTS!

OPEN 'EM!

HELLO, JESSE.

YOU'RE GOING TO BE A GOOD LITTLE BOY FROM NOW ON, AREN'T YOU? NO MORE FILTHY WORDS? NO MORE DISOBEDIENCE?

BECAUSE OTHERWISE IT'S THE COFFIN AGAIN, JESSE. *BAD BOYS* ALWAYS GET THE COFFIN AROUND THESE PARTS.

UH... AA--

GOOD BOY? MM? YES?

YUH--

YUH.

GOOD BOY.

I GUESS IT WAS ROUND THEN I GREW TO BELIEVE IN THE LORD. MOM WAS GONE, SO WAS DAD. GRAN'MA'S PAGE A DAY BEGAN TO TELL.

I KNEW *SHE* DIDN'T LOVE ME, JODY AN' T.C., I DOUBT THEY EVEN KNEW THE DAMN WORD. BUT EVERY DAY I'D HAVE THE BIBLE TELLIN' ME *GOD* LOVED ME...

WELL, I THOUGHT.

LONG AS SOMEBODY DID.

AN' THERE WAS STILL BILLY-BOB. I KNOW HE HAD THE EYE AN' ALL, BUT HE WAS STILL MY FRIEND AN' BELIEVE ME : WAY THINGS WERE, THAT MEANT A *LOT*.

HE WAS DUE TO MARRY HIS SISTER WHEN HE TURNED SIXTEEN, AN' HE JUST COULDN'T WAIT...

YOU'LL BE MY BEST MAN, WON'T YOU, JESSE?

SURE. I MEAN, I GUESS.

I GOTTA ASK GRAN'MA FOR TIME OFF MY STUDIES. GOTTA BE READY FOR PREACHER SCHOOL, END OF SUMMER. AN' JODY'S GOT ME WORKIN' REAL HARD AROUND THE PLACE...

MM.

JESSE? SURE WAS MORE FUN WHEN YOU DIDN'T HAVE TO ASK PERMISSION SO MUCH, HUH?

'COURSE I'LL BE YOUR BEST MAN, BILLY-BOB.

SO THERE WAS STILL A LITTLE HOPE IN THE WORLD, SO LONG AS I HAD A FRIEND.

CAME THE DAY THAT T.C. FUCKED THE CHICKEN...

FIRST THING I DID WHEN MY ARM GOT BETTER, I SLIPPED AWAY TO SEE BILLY-BOB'S FOLKS. WASN'T TOO FAR. I'D BE BACK BEFORE GRAN'MA SAW I WAS GONE.

I FIGURED.

DEAD? IN THE SWAMP?

BILLY-BAWWB!

I'M REAL SORRY, MA'AM. WASN'T A THING I COULD DO.

I BET. YOU L'ANGELLES, ALL YOU DO IS CAUSE MISERY TO FOLKS. ALWAYS BEEN THAT WAY.

SNAKES IN THE NIGHT, THAT'S WHAT YOU ARE.

MY NAME AIN'T L'ANGELLE, MA'AM.

I DON'T CARE WHAT YOUR DAMN NAME IS.

YOUR DAMN FAMILY MURDERED MY BOY, YOU THAT'S S'POSED TO BE HIS BEST FRIEND! KNOWIN' YOU'S ABOUT THE WORST THING BILLY-BOB COULDA HAD HAPPEN TO HIM!

GET OUTTA OUR HOME, YOU SON OF A BITCH!

LITTLE EXTRA KICK IN THE TEETH LIKE THAT, THAT'LL GET TO YOU.

LIKE WHEN THEY'RE DRAGGIN' MOM AWAY AN' GRAN'MA SAYS *LOOK WHAT YOU DID*, OR JODY CALLIN' ME A CRYBABY WHEN HE SHOT MY DAD. SAME AGAIN.

AN' THE WAY I SAW IT, AS LONG AS I STAYED IN ANGELVILLE, IT WAS JUST GONNA KEEP RIGHT ON HAPPENING.

ANGELVILLE KILLED 'EM ALL. ANYONE ELSE I EVER CARED ABOUT, IT WAS GONNA KILL THEM TOO--

AW NO, BABY--!

JUST GO ON.

WELL... I GOT SCARED JUST FOR A SECOND--OF GRAN'MA, OF JODY, EVEN OF *LEAVIN'*. IT MIGHT'VE BEEN HELL, BUT IT WAS STILL THE ONLY PLACE I REALLY KNEW.

FUCK IT, I SAID.

I'M NEVER GOIN' BACK.

LONG TIME BEFORE, MY MOM PROBABLY SAID THE SAME DAMN THING.

68

THIS IS... JUST BEFORE YOU MET ME, RIGHT?

YEAR OR TWO BEFORE.

I MADE IT AS FAR AS BEAUMONT BEFORE I REALIZED I DIDN'T EVEN KNOW WHAT I WAS DOIN'. ALL I KNEW WAS, ANGELVILLE WAS EAST AN' TEXAS WAS WEST.

NO CONTEST.

AN' YOU CAN FIND PLENTY TO DO, YOU'VE JUST TURNED SEVENTEEN.

KIND OF WEIRD.

I'M AWAY FROM HOME FOR ABOUT THE FIRST TIME, AN' ALL I REALLY KNOW ABOUT THE WORLD IS WHAT I'VE SEEN ON TV...

SO IT'S A GOOD THING ALL YOU WANT TO DO IS DRINK AND FUCK.

ANYHOW. JODY'D SPENT HIS TEENS ON THE LLANO, UP WHERE THEY AIN'T QUITE READY TO GIVE UP BEIN' COWBOYS YET. KNEW AS MUCH ABOUT HORSES AS HE DID ABOUT ENGINES.

GUESS I PICKED UP QUITE A BIT OF BOTH, WATCHIN' THE SON OF A BITCH.

GOT SO I COULD WORK A COUPLE WEEKS UP IN LUBBOCK, THEN COME SOUTH TO AUSTIN OR SAN ANTONE AN' PARTY AWAY EVERY CENT. HELL, I WAS --

EXIT

YOU WERE A COCKY LITTLE BASTARD, JESSE.

RRR.

I HAD TO HAVE YOU.

70

WHAT *IS* HE DOING WITH THAT SKINNY SLUT...?

NEVER DID COTTON MUCH TO ZOE, DID YOU?

NOPE.

GUESS THAT MADE IT EASIER TO STEAL ME FROM HER.

GOT YOUR LIGHTER?

SURE, BABY--

MM.

IF ONLY MOM'D WARNED ME ABOUT THE OLDER WOMAN...

THREE YEARS OLDER. NOT EXACTLY MRS. ROBINSON.

WELL, EXIT ZOE. ENTER MAD LOVE, HOT SEX, AN' OUR GUILTY LITTLE SECRET...

ARE YOU CRAZY --OH GOD...!

MMMM...

HOW'M I S'POSED TO--

GET OUTTA THERE! GET YOUR ASSES *OUT!*

SHIIIT!!

YOU GODDAMNED LITTLE FUCKS!!

ALL THE TIME WE WERE TOGETHER, AN' MY ABIDING MEMORIES ARE GRAND THEFT AUTO--

CHRIST, JESSE. FIVE YEARS ON AND THAT STILL GETS TO ME LIKE IT WAS YESTERDAY.

THIS NEXT PART, BABY, THIS IS GONNA ANSWER ALL YOUR QUESTIONS. WHAT I'VE BEEN LEADING UP TO, WHY I LEFT YOU, ANNVILLE...

THIS IS THAT MORNIN' IN JULY, WHEN WE JUST GOT INTO PHOENIX.

SELLIN' HOT CARS PAID BETTER'N BUSTIN' MY ASS IN NORTH TEXAS, BUT YOU'LL RECALL WE COULDN'T MANAGE OUR MONEY WORTH A DAMN...

THIRTY DOLLARS.

MM?

HOW MUCH CASH WE'VE GOT LEFT. STEAL SOMETHING PRICEY TONIGHT, WILL YOU?

GONNA DO THAT ANYWAY.

WANNA HIT CALIFORNIA IN STYLE.

YOU TOOK SOME FINDIN', BOY.

I'LL MAKE THIS REAL SIMPLE. YOU COME WITH US NICE AN' QUIET AN' DON'T MAKE NO FUSS, OR I'LL SHOOT HER THROUGH THE FUCKIN' HEAD.

MY GIRLFRIENDS ASKED ME WHAT'S HE LIKE AN' I SAID, HE'S KIND OF SHY...

BUT THAT'S THE KINDA GIRL I AM HE'S MY KINDA GUY--

JESSE?

JESSE, I--I'VE BEEN *HATING YOU* FOR FIVE YEARS FOR *NO REASON* AT *ALL!*

WHY DIDN'T *YOU TELL ME*...?

'CAUSE I'M A *FUCKIN'* IDIOT.

I DIDN'T WANT TO HAVE TO EXPLAIN ABOUT GRAN'MA AN' ANGELVILLE, ALL THAT SHIT. FIGURED YOU'D THINK I WAS SOME KINDA FUCKIN' FREAK...

WAY YOU LOOKED AT ME A COUPLE TIMES THERE, MAYBE I WASN'T FAR WRONG.

AFTER THAT-- I HATE TO SAY IT, BUT I JUST WENT BELLY-UP AN' QUIT.

YOU COULDN'T ESCAPE ANGELVILLE, *EVER*. YOU FOUGHT IT, IT BEAT THE SHIT OUT OF YOU. YOU RAN, IT JUST DRAGGED YOU BACK.

GRAN'MA HAD JODY KICK MY ASS BUT GOOD, AN' I DIDN'T LIFT A FINGER TO STOP HIM. I DID A *MONTH* IN THE COFFIN...

AN' THEN AT LAST--AT *LONG* LAST--

77

I TRULY LEARNED TO LOVE THE LORD.

THAT'S WHAT GOD'S THERE FOR.

WHEN YOU'RE BEATEN, WHEN YOU HAVEN'T AN OUNCE OF FIGHT LEFT IN YOU, WHEN YOU JUST CAN'T HACK IT BY YOURSELF ANYMORE:

YOU TURN TO JESUS OR YOU STICK A FUCKIN' GUN IN YOUR MOUTH.

I WAS HAPPY. GRAN'MA WAS HAPPY. HELL, ALL OF US WERE FUCKIN' *DELIRIOUS.*

SHE PULLED A FEW STRINGS AN' GOT ME PUSHED THROUGH THE MINISTRY IN RECORD TIME. COUPLE OF YEARS AN' REVEREND JESSE CUSTER WAS DOING THE LORD'S WORK AMONG THE GOOD PEOPLE OF *ANNVILLE*...

AN' THEN, ONE NIGHT NOT SO LONG AGO:

FUCK 'EM.

COUPLE OF YEARS OF *THAT,* AN' HE WAS PUTTIN' AWAY A BOTTLE OF J.D. A NIGHT.

FUCK 'EM *ALL.*

TULIP...

I AM THE BIGGEST, DUMBEST, STUPIDEST FUCK-UP IN THE WHOLE GODDAMN WORLD FOR NOT BEIN' STRAIGHT WITH YOU, AN' I HAVE NO RIGHT TO SAY THIS 'CAUSE I'VE GOT YOU KILLED BY BRINGIN' YOU HERE:

AN' I'LL LOVE YOU UNTIL THE END OF THE WORLD.

GOOD MORNING, JESSE.

BUT I SWEAR TO GOD I LOVE YOU.

JODY?

GLENN FABRY '95

BOYS.

MISS L'ANGELLE.

WANT ME TO GO GET THE COFFIN READY, MA'AM?

...NO.

NO THANK YOU, T.C. I DON'T THINK THAT'LL BE NECESSARY. PERHAPS YOU COULD FETCH A SHEET TO WRAP THE BODY IN, INSTEAD?

SURE THING.

MA'AM?

OH, LOOK AT HIM, JODY.

JUST LOOK AT HIM. HE'S BEATEN. HE'S LOST. THE LAST SPARK OF WILL AND WICKEDNESS IN HIM IS GONE FOREVER.

AND THE ONLY THING THAT COULD HAVE KEPT HIM FROM BECOMING MINE AGAIN...

IS LYING OVER THERE ON THE FLOOR.

I DUNNO, MISS L'ANGELLE. WE FIGURED HE WAS BEAT A COUPLE TIMES BEFORE, DIDN'T WE?

THAT WAS DIFFERENT.

HE HAS NOTHING TO RUN AWAY TO, THIS TIME. NO FURY TO SPUR HIM ON. NO *GENESIS* TO SEND HIM ON HIS UNHOLY QUEST... AT LEAST AS FAR AS HE KNOWS.

YOU MEAN THAT VOICE OF HIS? YOU NOTICE HIM TRYIN' IT THERE, EVEN WHEN IT WOULDN'T WORK ON ME BEFORE?

IT'LL NEVER WORK ON US.

WHICH REMINDS ME: IF YOU AND T.C. WOULD BE SO GOOD AS TO CARRY THE BODY UP TO MY BEDROOM--AND DON'T DALLY THERE. LEAVE THE ROOM AT ONCE.

WHATEVER YOU DO, DON'T LEAVE T.C. ALONE WITH HER.

OH, I DUNNO THAT HE'D DO IT WITH A DEAD GIRL...

JUST IN CASE.

THEN YOU CAN TAKE MY GRANDSON TO HIS QUARTERS --AND I'LL BET YOU FIFTY YANKEE DOLLARS YOU CAN LEAD HIM LIKE A NEWBORN LAMB.

I'M GLAD THIS IS OVER. I KNOW I'VE OUTLIVED MY THREE-SCORE AND TEN, JUST TO ENSURE THE FUTURE OF THIS GRAND OLD PLACE...

IT'LL BE A RELIEF TO REST AT LAST, JODY.

....

YES, MA'AM.

WHAT...?

WELL, YA AIN'T DONE TOO WELL BY *ME* NOW, HAVE YA?

HOW THE HELL CAN YOU STAND THERE AN' *SAY THAT?* YOU KNOW I'VE LOOKED UP TO YOU SINCE I WAS THREE YEARS OLD...!

SINCE--

SINCE *TRUE GRIT.*

FILL YOUR HAND, YOU SONUVABITCH!

OH YEAH? SO HOW COME I LISTENED TA YA TELL YER GIRL YER STORY--

--AN' I DIDN'T HEAR MY NAME MENTIONED *ONCE?*

UH...

JESUS, I DUNNO. IT'S KIND OF DIFFICULT TO TALK ABOUT IT WHEN I AIN'T TOO SURE OF THE DETAILS MYSELF...

UH-HUH?

IT'S...LOOK, IT AIN'T THE FACT THAT WE TALK THAT BOTHERS ME AS SUCH. LIKE I SAY, IT'S THE DETAILS.

LIKE YOU, YOU KNOW, YOU DIED IN NINETEEN SEVENTY-NINE --BUT YOU STARTED SHOWIN' UP WITH ME FOUR YEARS EARLIER, RIGHT AFTER MY DADDY WAS KILLED.

AN' IT SEEMS LIKE I'M THE ONLY ONE CAN SEE YOU ...AN' HELL, I AIN'T UNGRATEFUL, BUT EXCEPT FOR FILLIN' ME IN ON THE **SAINT**-- YOU AIN'T **REALLY** EVER TOLD ME ANYTHING I COULDN'T FIGURE OUT MYSELF...

AM I RIGHT?

WELL PARDON **ME** ALL TO HELL! LOOKED TA ME LIKE YER BACK WAS TA THE WALL! NEVER FIGURED IT WAS TIME FER **DAMNFOOL** QUESTIONS!

SO ... SO THIS IS ...

NO, WAIT A MINUTE, WHAT KIND OF HEAVEN IS *THIS*? IT LOOKS LIKE SOMEONE'S BEDROOM AND--

AND I DON'T *FEEL* DEAD.

YOU ARE NOT.

I TOLD YOU, CHILD. I AM THE *RESURRECTION*.

I AM THE WAY AND THE TRUTH AND THE LIGHT. I AM THE ALPHA AND THE OMEGA, AND THE BRIGHT MORNING STAR.

I AM THE LORD YOUR GOD.

OH YES: I AM YOUR FATHER IN HEAVEN, CHILD. I LOVE YOU AS I LOVE ALL MY CHILDREN ON THIS EARTH.

I WANT YOU TO LIVE, AND I WANT YOU TO LOVE ME:

94

AND I WANT *JESSE* TO LOVE ME TOO.

GO TO HIM FOR ME, TULIP. TELL HIM HOW I LOVE HIM SO, THAT I HAVE BROUGHT YOU BACK. TELL HIM THERE IS NO *NEED* FOR HIM TO SEARCH THE WORLD FOR ME, OR WONDER WHY I WANDER FAR FROM PARADISE.

ALL I ASK IS THAT HE TRUST ME ONCE AGAIN.

TRUST YOU...?

IS THAT SO MUCH FOR THE CREATOR TO ASK OF HIS CREATION?

HIS GRANDMOTHER AND HER COHORTS ARE EVIL PEOPLE. TELL HIM I HAVE RESTORED HIS POWER OVER THEM, THAT HE MAY JUDGE THEM AS HE SEES FIT. THEN BOTH OF YOU MAY GO IN PEACE.

NOW. I HAVE DEALT MORE THAN FAIRLY WITH HIM, TULIP. HIS LOVE AND TRUST ARE BUT A LITTLE PRICE TO ASK.

WHAT DO YOU THINK HE'D SAY TO ME, MM?

I THINK HE'D SAY *CUT THE SHIT.*

SHIT...

BUT ANY TIME IT LOOKED LIKE YA'D SHOW A LITTLE SPARK--

LAST BOTTLE.

YA JUST DROWNED IT.

THAT'S WHY I COULD HARDLY BELIEVE IT, YOU COMIN' BACK THE WAY YOU DID.

HELL, SOME GOOD IT DID ME! YER GITTIN' READY TA THROW IT ALL AWAY AGAIN!

YA ALWAYS LET 'EM BEAT YA, DAMMIT--AN' WHAT ARE THEY BUT A ...MEAN OL' GAL FROM A LONG LINE OF SIMILAR, BACKED BY A BUNCHA TRASH?

WAIT A SECOND HERE, THEY AIN'T BUT ANYTHING. GRAN'MA'S FUCKIN' EVIL INCARNATE AS FAR AS I CAN SEE, AN' EVERY TIME I TRY AN' FIGHT HER, SOMEONE CLOSE TO ME DIES--

THERE YA GO, GODDAMMIT!

THAT'S QUITTIN' TALK!

uh-huh.

WELL, WE DO IF THAT PIECE OF SHIT JEEP DOESN'T DIE ON US. THAT HAPPENS, IT'S GONNA TAKE US A LITTLE WHILE LONGER.

GOD, YOU'RE GORGEOUS...!

HUH?

I SAID YOU'RE *GORGEOUS*. EVERY MINUTE OF THE DAY, I WANT TO REACH OVER AND TOUCH YOU TO MAKE SURE YOU'RE REAL.

YOUR GREAT BIG EYES AND YOUR BIG SMUG GRIN AND YOUR BLACK, BLACK HAIR.

AND YOUR JAMES DEAN POSE YOU DO SO *FUCKING WELL*--!

ALL IN THE MARLBOROS.

I'VE NEVER HAD SO MUCH FUN WITH ANYONE BEFORE, YOU KNOW THAT? IF I EVER LOST YOU--

CHRIST, I THINK I'D GROW OLD OVERNIGHT IF I LOST YOU.

I AIN'T GOIN' ANYWHERE, BABY. I LOVE YOU.

MM...?

UNTIL THE END OF THE WORLD.

LITTLE JESSE?

LITTLE JESSE?

HHHHHRIGHT.

NO MORE QUITTIN'. I'M GONNA GO GET GRAN'MA AN' JODY AN' THE REST'VE THAT MOTHERFUCKIN' VERMIN, AN' I'M GONNA STAMP 'EM INTO THE SHIT THEY CAME FROM.

AN' THEN I'M GOIN' BACK TO LOOKIN' FOR GOD, AN' WHEN I FIND HIM--

HE BETTER HAVE A FUCKIN' GOOD EXCUSE.

GLAD TA HEAR IT, PILGRIM. 'CAUSE THERE'S A LITTLE GIRL LYIN' DEAD OUT THERE THAT NEEDS AVENGIN'.

YOU KIN TALK THE TALK--

IT IS NOT *FOR YOU* TO UNDERSTAND MY WAYS, TULIP. ALL YOU NEED DO IS ACCEPT.

AND TRUST.

THAT'S FUNNY, THAT'S EXACTLY WHAT I USED TO HEAR IN SUNDAY SCHOOL.

I DIDN'T LIKE IT THEN, EITHER. I'VE NEVER BEEN ONE FOR BLIND FAITH.

I'VE GOT MY OWN THEORY: I DON'T THINK YOU'RE SUCH HOT SHIT. I RECKON YOU'RE SCARED OF MEETING JESSE FACE TO FACE--

AND I NOTICE YOU'VE QUIT THE FUCKING SILLY SPECIAL EFFECTS, TOO...

THAT IS QUITE ENOUGH!

I AM LEAVING.

YOU GO TO JESSE CUSTER, AND YOU TELL HIM THIS HAS BEEN A *WARNING*. YOU TELL HIM THAT UNLESS HE FORGETS THIS RIDICULOUS ATTEMPT TO HUNT ME DOWN, THINGS WILL BE *MUCH WORSE* THE NEXT TIME.

I AM A LOVING GOD, TULIP--

BUT *DON'T PUSH IT.*

FUCK COMMUNISM

FUCK YOU, GRAN'MA.

FUCK YOU AN' ALLA YOUR MONSTERS.

GLENN FABRY 96

JESSE, WHERE *DID* YOU GET THAT LIGHTER...?

JOHN WAYNE GAVE IT TO MY DADDY AT KHE SANH.

uh...

FIGURE JODY TOOK IT WHEN HE SHOT HIM. ANYWAY, SINCE WHEN DID YOU TAKE UP SMOKIN' CIGARETTES?

MY DAD STARTED ME ON MY FOURTH BIRTHDAY. I USED TO QUIT ALL THE TIME, THEN FOR GOOD A COUPLE OF YEARS BACK.

BUT I FIGURED WITH EVERYTHING I'VE BEEN THROUGH RECENTLY, I DUNNO, I SORT OF OWED MYSELF THE LUXURY OF FALLING INTO AN OLD BAD HABIT...

COULDN'T HELP NOTICE YOU WENT BACK TO EATIN' MEAT.

FILTHY PIG.

TULIP?

MM?

I KINDA SKIPPED THIS BEFORE, 'CAUSE I FIGURED YOU MIGHTN'T WANNA TALK ABOUT IT--

BUT WHAT WAS IT LIKE GETTIN' SHOT THROUGH THE HEAD?

138

... IT WASN'T REALLY *LIKE* ANYTHING. I DIDN'T FEEL IT AT THE TIME, I JUST HEARD THIS *BANG* BEFORE EVERYTHING WENT BLACK--

THEN WHITE...

AND THEN HE WAS STANDING THERE IN FRONT OF ME.

THE *GOOD FUCKIN' LORD...!*

LIKE TO KNOW WHAT KINDA LOVING GOD IT IS SICS *GRAN'MA* AN' HER FUCKS ON US, AN' LETS YOU GO THROUGH WHAT YOU DID JUST TO PROVE HIS *GODDAMN* POINT--

I TELL YOU, I CATCH UP LIKE I'M PLANNIN' ON DOIN', HE'S GONNA HAVE A WHOLE LOTTA FUCKIN' EXPLAININ' TO DO.

HE KNOWS IT, TOO.

I THINK HE'S SCARED OF YOU.

I MEAN, I DON'T KNOW IF IT'S BECAUSE HE'S NOT AS POWERFUL AS HE'D LIKE TO BE...ONE MINUTE HE'S GOT THIS FIREWORKS DISPLAY GOING ON, LIKE YOU KIND OF *IMAGINE* THE SECOND COMING WOULD LOOK--AND THE NEXT HE'S THIS LITTLE OLD MAN SO, JESUS, SO *DULL* I CAN'T EXACTLY REMEMBER HIS FACE...

OR MAYBE IT'S BECAUSE HE JUST CAN'T MAKE UP HIS MIND. HE REALLY WAS ANXIOUS FOR ME TO THINK HE WAS A GOOD GUY, YOU KNOW?

WHICHEVER IT IS, IT SOUNDS LIKE WE GOT HIM ON THE RUN.

SO WHAT WILL YOU DO WHEN YOU GET THE ALMIGHTY BY THE BALLS?

SQUEEZE.

I DUNNO, DARLIN'. I FIGURE HE'S GOT WAY TOO MANY FOLKS PUTTIN' THEIR FAITH IN HIM JUST TO WALK OUT ON 'EM LIKE THAT.

HE OWES EVERY DAMN ONE OF US, YES HE DOES...

DON'T YOU GO GETTING OBSESSED ON ME, JESSE CUSTER. NOW I'VE GOT YOU BACK, I WANT ENOUGH TIME TO DEVOUR YOU AT MY LEISURE.

DIDN'T I PROMISE YOU A COUPLE WEEKS OFF? DIDN'T I DELIVER?

YOU DID.

HEY, YOU KNOW WHO I CALLED LAST NIGHT?

WHO?

"OI CAN'T COME TO THE FOCKIN' PHONE AT THE MINUTE, 'CAUSE OI'M PISSED OUTTA ME SKULL AT FISTED SISTER'S ON DIVISADERO. YEH CAN LEAVE A MESSAGE AFTER THE BEEP, YEH BOLLICKS. **BEEEP**"

I COMPLETELY FORGOT HE WAS IN SAN FRANCISCO...

MORE'N LIKELY HE HAS, TOO.

DON'T YOU WANNA SEE HIM?

SURE. IT'S JUST...LOOK, I KNOW YOU TWO REALLY HIT IT OFF, AND I'M GLAD. BUT I DON'T THINK HE TAKES ME VERY SERIOUSLY, JESSE.

AND THERE *IS* THE BLOOD-DRINKING THING...

HE FELT LIKE SHIT WHEN YOU GOT HURT IN NEW YORK.

YEAH.

FORGET IT.

GOD, IT'S JUST SO GOOD TO FEEL LIKE THIS AGAIN. TO WANT TO KISS YOU EVERY MINUTE I SEE YOU...

YOU MAKE ME FEEL YOUNG, YOU KNOW THAT?

I TELL YOU, WITH ANGELVILLE OFF MY ASS AN' YOU BACK IN MY ARMS: I NEVER IN MY LIFE FELT SO DAMN *FREE*.

LOVE ME, CUSTER?

UNTIL THE END OF THE WORLD.

141

AND HOW ARE WE TODAY?

I'M--

I HAVE BEEN SEEING SOMETHING OF YOUR SAN FRANCISCO, AND HAVE TO ADMIT TO QUITE LIKING IT...

I'M SURE IT QUITE LIKES YOU TOO, THIERRY.

I READ YOUR PERSONNEL FILES, FEATHERSTONE. SUCH A SHAME SO FEW OF THEM ARE BELIEVERS...

I KNOW. I'VE ALWAYS REGRETTED THE LACK OF FAITH TO BE FOUND AMONG MERCENARIES AND ASSASSINS, THIERRY.

IN THE GRAIL, FEATHERSTONE, WE PREFER TO EMPLOY CHRISTIANS WHEN WE CAN.

ON THAT NOTE: AN ADDITIONAL OPERATIVE IS ARRIVING TODAY, TO ASSIST ON THE CUSTER INVESTIGATION. HIS NAME IS STARR.

BOSH?

GERMAN.

UN BOCHE...

A KRAUT.

143

M'SIEUR STARR?

MY NAME IS POUISSIN. PLEASE GET IN.

FEATHERSTONE AND HOOVER?

YE--

CORRECT.

I UNDERSTAND YOU'RE HERE TO--

MR. POUISSIN, ARE YOU AWARE THAT THESE TWO ARE PART OF A CONSPIRACY *WITHIN* THE GRAIL ITSELF? A PLAN TO DESTROY WHAT IT HAS PROTECTED FOR TWO THOUSAND YEARS?

'PRECIATE THE LOAN, CASS. IT'S ALL THERE.

CHEERS. DID YEH REALLY ROB A BANK, AYE? DID YEH USE YER *WORD*?

YEP. STILL REMEMBERED TO SAY PLEASE.

GUY BEHIND ME IN THE QUEUE HEARS THIS, SEES THE TELLER HAND ME TEN GRAND IN USED BILLS -- SO HE TRIES THE SAME GODDAMN THING. HE'S STILL SCREAMIN' *GIVE ME TEN THOUSAND DOLLARS PLEASE!* WHEN I'M WALKIN' OUT THE DOOR.

YOU THINK THAT'S GOOD, THE MANAGER GAVE ME HIS TRANS AM.

I'M GLAD TO SEE THAT ABSOLUTE POWER'S CORRUPTIN' ABSOLUTELY.

MM. WELL, FIRST OF ALL, WE HAD A BAD TIME IN THE SOUTH, AN' TULIP GOT IT MUCH WORSE'N I DID. FIGURED SHE COULD USE A LITTLE HIGH LIFE.

AN' SECOND OF ALL: FUCK IT.

AYE, WELL, THAT'S ALWAYS BEEN MY ATTITUDE --HERE!

IS THAT LAUREL AN' HARDY?

150

...AN' JUST AS THEIR BOAT'S COMIN' IN, ALL THE CHURCH BELLS START RINGIN', RIGHT? AN' THEY GO-- deedee-deedee, deedee-deedee... ♪

♪ deedeedeedee, deedeedeedee! deedee-deedee, deedee-deedee, deedee-deedee DA-DA!! ♪

AN' STAN TURNS TO OLLIE, AN' THEY'RE BOTH CRYIN' THEIR FUCKIN' EYES OUT, AN' HE SAYS, "THEY DON'T LIKE US--"

"THEY LOVE US."

AH, JAYSIS. HERE, BLESSED ARE THE PEACE-MAKERS, WHA'?

MATTER OF FACT, I STARTED THAT ONE FOR YOU.

YOU BEEN--MM--KINDA TWITCHY ALL NIGHT, LIKE YOU WERE TRYIN' TOO HARD TO BE HAPPY. I GOT THE FEELIN' YOU MIGHT HAVE A LITTLE FRUSTRATION TO USE UP ON SOMEONE.

AYE, YEH WERE RIGHT.

I BURIED ME GIRL-FRIEND LAST WEEK.

BOYS WILL BE BOYS

I CAN PROBABLY JUST YANK THE FRONT OFF--AW, *FUCK.*

WHAT?

SHE'S WIRED THIS TO BLOW UP IF ANYONE FRIGS ABOUT WI' IT. AN I'M THE FUCKIN' EEJIT TAUGHT HER EXPLOSIVES.

AW FUCK, WE'RE NOT GETTIN' IN HERE WITHOUT THE BASTARD COMBINATION...

YOU SEEN THIS?

HRRSSSS

SSSSSS

JAYSIS, THE COLLAR--!

I BET THAT'S IT-- *AAH!*

SON OF A BITCH!

HERE, HOUL' ON! TRY THE WORD ON THE FUCKER!

GODDAMN RIGHT...

C'MERE, YOU FAT PIECE OF SHIT!

HRRRSS!

DOESN'T SPEAK AMERICAN.

♪ TIME FLIES BY WHEN ♫ YOU'RE THE DRIVER OF A TRAIN, AND YOU STAND ON THE FOOTPLATE, THERE AND BACK AGAIN... ♪

MORNING, HARCOURT.

MORNING, MY LORD.

DIRK! LORD JESUS WANTS TO PARK HIS BICYCLE!

HNN--

HOW GO THE PREPARATIONS, HARCOURT?

WITHOUT A HITCH, MY LORD. EXCEPT...*ah*...

EXCEPT?

STILL NO NEWS FROM BOB AND FREDDY.

HOW DREARY.

WELL, THEY'D BETTER COME UP WITH THE NARCOTICS IN QUESTION. NOTHING GIVES AN ORGASM THAT JE-NE-SAIS-QUOI! LIKE A NICE SYRINGE OF HEROIN...

THIS IS GOING TO BE ONE OF MY BEST PARTIES EVER--

AND I DON'T WANT A *SINGLE* GUEST TO LEAVE FEELING ANYTHING LESS THAN *THOROUGHLY* FUCKED.

er... PARDON ME...

ONE FOR YOU, ANGEL.

ARE YOU LADIES PROSTITUTES, BY ANY CHANCE?

NO, WE'RE ASTRONAUTS. WE'RE GOING UP ON THE NEXT SHUTTLE.

WHAT THE FUCK DOES IT LOOK LIKE, FOR CHRISSAKES...?

AH. WELL, THE THING IS, I--

I HAVE TO ENGAGE THE SERVICES OF A PROSTITUTE, YOU SEE. I'M SORRY IF I SEEM, um... BUT I DON'T REALLY HAVE A GREAT DEAL OF EXPERIENCE...

NO SHIT.

YOUR LUCKY DAY, MISTER. I KNOW SOME PEOPLE BE ONLY TOO HAPPY TO HELP YOU. HERE--

WHY DON'T YOU GIVE 'EM A CALL?

WELL... THAT'S VERY KIND OF YOU...

hmp!

ALLEN
INVESTIGATORS
HAIGHT ST.
CO CA 94113
6233226

OH, YOU BAD, GIRL! THAT'S THE CRUELEST MOTHER-FUCKIN' THING I EVER SEEN!

YEAH, LIKE YOU TRIED TO STOP ME.

HELLO?

YES, SPEAKING. YOU WHAT?

YOU WANT TO *ENGAGE OUR SERVICES?* WHAT, FOR YOURSELF?

OH NO! NO, IT'S NOT FOR ME! I'M SUPPOSED TO BE ARRANGING THIS FOR SOMEONE ELSE--

AH, YOU WANT SOMEBODY *DONE!* AH, YOU SHOULD'VE SAID SO IN THE FIRST PLACE!

RIGHT, YEAH... GOT IT...

OKAY, UP THE BACK ALLEY--AND ISN'T THAT APPROPRIATE--AT THE RITZ-CARLTON. TEN-THIRTY SHARP, AYE.

NO PROBLEM. BELIEVE ME, MATE:

HE WON'T EVEN KNOW WHAT HIT HIM!

...AND YOU'RE SURE YOU SPECIFIED THE ALLEY? IT'LL BE AS --*SORDID* AS POSSIBLE?

WELL DONE, HOOVER.

YOU WERE TELLING ME ABOUT CUSTER...?

MM? OH, YES.

AS I TOLD YOU, THE MASSES WILL WANT TO SEE MIRACLES...

171

VIGILANCE BEGAN ON CUSTER AFTER A SERIES OF INCIDENTS IN AND AROUND ANNVILLE, TEXAS, ROUGHLY SIX MONTHS AGO. TWO HUNDRED PEOPLE DIED WHEN CUSTER'S CHURCH EXPLODED, ALTHOUGH HIS OWN BODY WAS NEVER FOUND.

OVER A DOZEN SHERIFF'S DEPUTIES DIED OF GUNSHOT WOUNDS THROUGHOUT THE NEXT THIRTY-SIX HOURS. SPECIAL AGENT DINNINGS OF THE F.B.I. CONCLUDED:

"CUSTER'S RIGHT IN THE MIDDLE OF ALL THIS SHIT. BUT HOW? AND WHY?"

"MY CONTACT IN DINNINGS' OFFICE REPORTS THAT HE HAS RELUCTANTLY CLOSED THE CASE--AT LEAST OFFICIALLY--UNDER ORDERS, AS THE RESULT OF A REPORT BY ONE JOHN TOOL OF THE N.Y.P.D. ...

"TOOL SPILLED HIS GUTS AT THE EMPTY PROMISE OF A PRETTY SMILE. HE SWEARS THAT CUSTER IS DEAD, WHICH I DON'T BELIEVE FOR A SECOND, BUT THAT HE HIMSELF WATCHED CUSTER KILL A MAN BY ORDERING HIM TO DIE--

"AND HANDED OVER HIS OWN SIDEARM, WHEN CUSTER ORDERED HIM TO DO SO."

AND YOU BELIEVE THIS?

I HAVE ANOTHER... SOURCE... ONE, IN FACT, THAT I TRUST IMPLICITLY. AN INDIVIDUAL IN NO POSITION TO LIE.

THEY CONFIRMED TOOL'S STATEMENT WITHOUT QUESTION.

172

HE COULD MAKE *ANYONE* DO *ANYTHING*?

IN THEORY.

SO YOU THINK HE'S IN SAN FRANCISCO...

NO. I'M HERE BECAUSE OF POUISSIN.

POUISSIN SAW THE LIST OF TROUBLESOME OPERATIVES I'D COMPILED, INCLUDING YOU WITH YOUR HALF-DOZEN QUERIES. HE SUSPECTED I WAS UP TO SOMETHING, BUT HE KNEW D'ARONIQUE ADMIRED ME AND THAT HE'D NEED *PROOF*...

HE CAME HERE BECAUSE HE HOPED YOU'D GIVE ME AWAY. YOU DIDN'T ACTUALLY KNOW MY NAME, BUT HIS DISCOVERY OF *ANY* CONSPIRACY WITHIN THE GRAIL WOULD HAVE ENDANGERED ME.

I THINK I SHOT HIM JUST IN TIME.

BUT POUISSIN WASN'T HERE OF HIS OWN ACCORD. D'ARONIQUE *SENT HIM* HERE AFTER CUSTER. FOLLOWING HIS CONSPIRACY THEORY WAS A PRIVATE SIDELINE.

POUISSIN, YOU SEE, COMMANDED THE ENTIRE CUSTER INVESTIGATION...

BUT HERR STARR, IF THE ALLFATHER HIMSELF PUT POUISSIN IN CHARGE OF IT...IF CUSTER IS REALLY *THAT* IMPORTANT...

I KNOW THIS SOUNDS INCREDIBLE, BUT--WELL, HAVE YOU CONSIDERED THAT D'ARONIQUE MIGHT HAVE REACHED THE SAME CONCLUSION YOU DID?

YOU *ARE* GOOD.

BUT WHY WOULD HE CONTINUE TO PROTECT THE CHILD, IF HE THOUGHT HE HAD A READY-MADE MESSIAH HERE? OH, HE *WANTS* CUSTER...BUT NOT FOR THAT.

I THINK IT MIGHT BE SOMETHING PERSONAL.

KNOCK IT OFF, CUSTER.

UH?

REALLY, I MEAN IT. YOU SMELL LIKE A DISTILLERY.

AND WHAT THE HELL HAPPENED TO YOUR FACE?

SELF-DEFENSE, BABY...

GET OFF--

WHUP!

NOT 'TIL YOU SHOWER, BOY.

NOW COME ON, WHAT HAVE YOU BEEN UP TO?

GOT DRUNK AND GOT IN A FIGHT.

uh-huh.

SLEPT AT CASS'S GIRLFRIEND'S.

YOU'RE KIDDING! DID YOU MEET HER?

NOPE. SHE O.D.'ED A COUPLE OF WEEKS BACK.

SHE HAD A SAFE FULL OF HEROIN CASS AN' I ONLY JUST FOUND OUT ABOUT. CASS WANTS TO FIND WHOEVER GAVE IT TO HER AN' BREAK HIS GODDAMN LEGS.

TOLD HIM I'D GIVE HIM A HAND.

YOU KNOW WHAT?

I THINK HE'S A BAD INFLUENCE ON YOU.

AHA HA HA HA HA!!

174

THE SUN DIDN'T GO DOWN FOR ANOTHER SIX HOURS! I FELT LIKE A RIGHT FUCKIN' EEJIT!

I SHOULDA SKINNED THAT GODDAMN CAT...

I WANT THOSE TWO BOLLICKSES THAT TOOK THE SMACK, AN' I WANT THIS DeSADE BASTARD THAT OWNS IT. THEY'D NO RIGHT PUTTIN' TEMPTATION IN GRETA'S WAY LIKE THAT.

JESUS, THAT'S PROBABLY THE FUCKIN' STUFF SHE DID HERSELF IN WITH!

HAVE YOU GOT A PICTURE OF HER?

EH?

GRETA, DO YOU HAVE LIKE A PHOTO OF HER, MAYBE?

NAH. I NEVER BOTHER WITH ALL THAT CARRY-ON.

SO HOW COME YOU GOT THAT ONE OF US LAST NIGHT?

WELL--

'SCUSE ME, HONEY...

J.D. AN' ICE, BECKS DARK--

ANAPINKMELON RAINBOWSTARBURST.

I'M SORRY?

A PINK MELON RAINBOW STARBURST.

OKEY-DOKEY.

WHY DON'T YOU GET ONE TOO, SURE? YEH'D MAKE A NICE WEE COUPLE.

I WAS WEARIN' A HAT LIKE THAT, I'D WANNA BE LAUGHIN', TOO.

177

SO THIS PHOTO THING...

AYE, I'LL HAVE TO GET IT DEVELOPED. JUST NIP TO THE BOG HERE.

I BET YOU TWENTY BUCKS WE NEVER GET TO SEE THAT PICTURE.

MM?

HE'LL KEEP IT.

I SAW HIM THIS MORNIN' WHEN HE TALKED ABOUT GRETA. HE DOESN'T LIKE FOLKS KNOWIN', BUT UNDERNEATH THAT I-COULD-GIVE-A-SHIT EXTERIOR IS ONE SOFT GODDAMN HEART...

I'LL BELIEVE IT WHEN I SEE IT.

KEEP THE CHANGE, HONEY.

THANKS, REVEREND!

THE PRETTIER THE WAITRESS, THE BIGGER THE TIP...

BULLSHIT--!

GUESS OLD HABITS DIE HARD, REVEREND.

HOPE YOU STRUCK A MATCH.

heh heh heh!

SO WHAT D'YOU MAKE OF STARR?

UMMM... I THINK HE'S COLD, RUTHLESS, AND MORE THAN A LITTLE PATRONIZING. ON THE OTHER HAND, I DOUBT HE'S EVER FAILED IN AN ASSIGNED TASK.

IF WE'RE GOING TO BE OPERATING *AGAINST* THE REST OF THE GRAIL, I'M DAMN GLAD WE'VE GOT HIM ON OUR SIDE.

AND HE *IS* A COMPLETE PROFESSIONAL. DO YOU KNOW HOW MANY TIMES I HAD TO SLAP POUSSIN'S HAND OFF MY ASS?

'SCUSE.

YEAH? OH.

UH-HUH... YEAH, LIKE I SAID.

WHAT?!

THAT WAS MY TAME COP ON THE S.F.P.D., YOU KNOW? IN DISPATCH?

AND?

THERE WAS A BRAWL IN A BAR ON HAIGHT LAST NIGHT. TWO GUYS PUT SEVEN OTHERS IN THE HOSPITAL, THEN WALKED AWAY.

YES? AND?

I PASSED THE CUSTER VIGILANCE THING ALONG TO ALL MY PEOPLE. THE COP SAYS THE BARMAID CLAIMS ONE OF THESE TWO WORE A MINISTER'S COLLAR--

AND HIS BUDDY WAS CALLING HIM *JESSE.*

179

GLENN FABRY '98

SO WHAT YOU THINK?

FUCKIN' DEADLY. I'M PARTICULARLY FOND OF THE TINTED WINDOWS...

SO IN THE SHADE LIKE THIS IS OKAY? IT'S GOTTA BE REAL SUNLIGHT TO HURT YOU?

AYE, BUT EVEN THIS HURTS A WEE BIT, YEH KNOW? IT'S ITCHY AS FUCK.

HOW'S OUL' TULIP?

SHE'S GREAT. SHE'S GOIN' SHOPPIN'.

THIRTEEN- ELEVEN HAIGHT... ...YEAH, WE GOT 'EM.

DARREN GORMLEY

B. GLOVER + F. ALLEN

LENNIE LAWRENCE

SHOPPIN', WHA'? THERE GOES YER ILL-GOTTEN GAINS.

SO LONG AS SHE'S HAPPY...

YEZ ARE OVER YER DIFFERENCES, I TAKE IT.

FOR GOOD.

BY THE WAY, HOW WERE WE GONNA HANDLE THIS?

WELL, I WANNA GET YER MAN DeSADE'S ADDRESS OUT'VE THEM, BUT APART FROM THAT... ...FUCK IT. LET'S JUST SMASH OUR WAY IN AN' BREAK THEIR FUCKIN' LEGS.

MM. COULD BE WE GOTTA GET IN LINE.

CRASHING THE PARTY

WHAT?

HE'S HERE. IN SAN FRANCISCO.

WE HAVE A POLICE REPORT ON A FIGHT IN A LOCAL BAR. ONE OF THE MEN INVOLVED WORE A MINISTER'S COLLAR AND ANSWERED TO "JESSE"--

AND ACCORDING TO THE BARMAID, HE HAD A *VOICE* THAT "TIME STOOD STILL FOR." SHE SAID *YOU COULDN'T HAVE HELPED BUT OBEY HIM*...

AND BY THE WAY, THE REPORT CAME COURTESY OF HOOVER.

OH, SO HE'S ACTUALLY GOOD FOR SOMETHING?

WHAT KIND OF *SHITHEAD* WOULD--

WHAT AM I-- AACCCHH --SUPPOSED TO KNOW ABOUT DEALING WITH PROSTITUTES?

SHUT UP.

IF I CAN'T KILL YOU, HOOVER, I'M GOING TO KILL THE *BAG OF SHIT* WHO DID THAT TO ME. I HAVE HIS ADDRESS.

AND YOU'RE COMING TOO.

WE'LL GET BACK TO CUSTER WHEN I RETURN. MEET ME AT THE CAR.

THAT-- THAT--

MOTHER-FUCKER?

FEATHERSTONE--!

WHAT THE FUCK *IS* THIS?

ALL YOURS.

NICE ONE. HERE, TELL US THIS: WHY DON'T YEH JUST USE YOUR WORD ON PEOPLE LIKE SHITE-FACE, INSTEAD OF BREAKIN' THEIR FUCKIN' ARSES?

WOULDN'T DO TO GET TOO RELIANT ON A THING LIKE THAT, CASS.

LIKE I FOUND OUT TO MY COST A WHILE BACK.

SO IT'S NOT JUST 'CAUSE YEH'RE A VIOLENT BASTARD, THEN?

DUNNO WHAT YOU MEAN.

EXCUSE ME?

I DUNNO WHO YOU TWO ASSHOLES THINK YOU ARE, BUT YOU'RE TAKIN' YOUR FUCKIN' LIVES IN YOUR HANDS! *NOBODY* DOES THIS SHIT TO ME!

YOU BETTER UNTIE ME *RIGHT NOW* OR YOU'RE GOIN' SWIMMIN' IN *FUCKIN'* CONCRETE, HEAR?

AH! ZE PRISONER IS READY FOR ZE INTERROGATION, JA? VOT IS YOUR NAME, ENGLANDER?

FUCK YOU--

YOU SCHWEINE!

OH DEAR.

UM... MR. STARR, I CAN EASILY HAVE SOMEONE ELSE DEAL WITH THIS. IT SEEMS A LITTLE BIT HANDS-ON FOR US...

HANDS-ON?

HOOVER, THANKS TO YOU I WON'T BE ABLE TO SIT DOWN WITHOUT *GASPING* FOR THE REST OF THE *FUCKING WEEK.* DON'T TALK TO ME ABOUT HANDS-ON.

I ASSUME YOU'RE ARMED?

YES SIR.

RIGHT, THE CARD THAT HOOKER GAVE YOU MENTIONED A "FREDDIE ALLEN" AS WELL -- AND I SUPPOSE I SHOULD THANK JESUS CHRIST ALMIGHTY YOU DIDN'T LET BOTH OF THEM LOOSE ON ME -- SO THAT MEANS THERE'S AT LEAST TWO OF THEM. WE'LL SHOOT THEM BOTH.

HMMMP! HMMMP!

HMMMP! HMM-MM-HMMMP!

190

MM. WHO TAUGHT YOU TO SHOOT?

I--I--I NEVER FIRED A GUN AT SOMEONE IN MY LIFE! I JUST DID IT WITH-OUT THINKING!

THAT SOUNDS LIKE YOU ALL RIGHT, HOOVER.

SHAME WE DIDN'T GET A DESCRIPTION OF CUSTER OUT OF HIM FIRST, MIND YOU. THE PICTURE I HAVE WAS TAKEN EIGHTEEN YEARS AGO.

WHO DO YOU USE FOR EXTREME SANCTIONS AROUND HERE?

THERE'S...THERE'S A DOZEN OR SO FREELANCERS IN TOWN, uh, MOSTLY EX-POLICE TACTICAL. NONE OF THEM KNOW WHO FEATHERSTONE AND I REALLY REPRESENT.

GET THEM ALL FOR TONIGHT. WE'LL STAKE OUT THIS PARTY, SEE IF CUSTER OR FREDDY SHOW UP.

IT COULD BE WE CAN KILL TWO BIRDS WITH ONE STONE HERE, HOOVER...

HOOVER?

OH, FOR GOD'S SAKE...!

WHAT D'YEH THINK, TULIP? D'YEH RECKON YER BOY-FRIEND MAYBE NEEDS A WEE CHAT WI' HIS INNER CHILD?

HMMM...

INNER CHILD?

OH AYE, YOU HATE THAT SORTA SHITE, DON'T YEH?

YEH MIGHT JUST BE IN DENIAL, BUT. MAYBE YEH NEED TO GET SOME DOWN-TIME AN REALLY TRY TO PROCESS YER ISSUES...

MM--THE WORST ONE I EVER HEARD-- AND I SWEAR THIS IS TRUE--WAS FROM THIS SANTA MONICA ASSHOLE I KNEW IN COLLEGE. THIS IS REAL, OKAY?

"I THINK IT'S TIME YOU TOOK A SWIM IN LAKE YOU."

NO...!

NOBODY FUCKIN' SAYS THAT!

HONEST INJUN.

JAYSIS, THERE'S SOME RIGHT FUCKIN' SELF-ABUSE EXPERTS IN THE WORLD, ISN'T THERE?

YEP.

RECKON MOST'VE 'EM ARE HERE TONIGHT.

198

I SEE WHAT YOU MEAN...

I USED TO GO TO BILL BURROUGHS' PARTIES, AN' I THOUGHT HE WAS A MADMAN--BUT THIS LOT BELONG ON THE FUCKIN' MOON!

IS THAT SPOCK...?

YOU KNEW WILLIAM BURROUGHS?

YOU GOT A PLAN?

AYE, HE PUT ME IN JUNKY. SORT OF.

EM...I DUNNO. WHAT D'YEH THINK YERSELF?

SPLIT UP, GO LOOKIN'. FIRST ONE OF US FINDS THESE ASSHOLES GOES TO FETCH THE OTHER TWO.

MEET UP BACK HERE IN, SAY, A HALF HOUR?

AYE, OKAY, WE'LL HAVE TO ASK AROUND, BUT I ONLY HEARD THEM TWO BASTARDS TALKIN', SO I DUNNO WHAT THEY LOOK LIKE.

WHAT ABOUT TULIP? WILL SHE BE OKAY ON HER OWN?

YOU COULD TRY ASKING HER, AND I CAN TAKE CARE OF MYSELF JUST FINE, THANKS.

HALF AN HOUR.

SORRY I FUCKIN' SPOKE...!

START INDOORS AN' WORK OUT, HUH?

DOES SHE STILL NOT LIKE ME, OR SOMETHIN'?

SHE LIKES YOU FINE.

IT'S MODERN WOMEN, IS ALL. THEY AIN'T JUST CHICKS NO MORE: THEY'RE CHICKS *IN THEIR OWN RIGHT...*

MODERN ME ARSE--

MY MA WAS IN HER OWN RIGHT, AN' THAT WAS NINETY FUCKIN' YEARS AGO. SHE USED TO BLATTER DA WI' THE FRYIN' PAN WHEN HE CAME HOME BOLLICKSED.

MATTER OF FACT, THIS REMINDS ME OF ANOTHER PET HATE...

YEH MEAN YEH'VE MORE'N JUST ONE?

YOU EVER RUN ACROSS THESE ASSHOLES WHO TALK ABOUT HAVIN' A PARTNER? NOT A GIRL OR BOYFRIEND, A *PARTNER*?

I MEAN, WAY I FIGURE IT, A PARTNER'S SOMEONE COVERS YOU WHEN YOU'RE BUSTIN' A CRACK HOUSE, OR TAKIN' A HERD UP THE OL' CHISHOLM TRAIL. *KOJAK* HAS A PARTNER.

A GUY'S SEEIN' A GIRL REGULAR, OR LIVIN' WITH HER, SHE *AIN'T* HIS PARTNER...

AYE, WELL SPEAKIN' OF THE OLD JISM TRAIL, WE'D BETTER START LOOKIN'. I'LL SEE YEH BACK OUTSIDE AN' WE CAN REASSESS OUR OPTIONS BILATERALLY, ALL RIGHT?

FUCK YOU.

LORD JESUS? EVERYONE KNOWS HIM! THIS IS HIS PARTY!

DESCRIBE HIM.

HE'S--HE'S TALL AND THIN, AND HE'S VERY PALE, AND HE'S VERY GOOD-LOOKING...I MEAN REALLY, YOU WILL KNOW HIM IF YOU SEE HIM...

HERE LOVE, DO YOU KNOW JESUS De--

HIT ME! BITE ME! I WANT YOU TO BITE ME!

heh heh heh! NO YEH DON'T!

ANYONE IN HERE KNOW--

DO IT! GO ON, YOU SLUTS! DO IT!

FORGET IT...

YOURS WOULD SEEM TO BE A RATHER ENLIGHTENED SORT OF CHURCH, REVEREND.

UNIQUE.

NOT MUCH POINT IN TRYING TO SHOCK YOU, MM?

I SUPPOSE THE REAL REASON WE DO THIS IS *EXCESS*: ITS SINGULAR PURSUIT, ALMOST AS AN END IN ITSELF.

THESE REVELLERS ARE THE PEOPLE'S HEROES AND MASTERS. THEIR POSTS REQUIRE AMBITION AND ENERGY ALL *WAY* ABOVE THE NORM, OR ELSE THEY WOULD NEVER HAVE CLIMBED SO HIGH.

THEIR OUTLETS FOR RELEASE ARE-- NATURALLY, THEREFORE-- EXCESSIVE.

NOTHIN' WRONG WITH THAT, SO LONG AS THEY AIN'T HURTIN' ANYBODY.

BUT THEN IT WOULDN'T *BE* EXCESS, WOULD IT? AFTER ALL, THE VERY REASON I THROW THESE LITTLE SOIREES IS--

WAIT A SECOND: THIS IS *YOUR* PARTY?

WHY, YES...

YOU'RE JESUS De SADE?

I ASSUMED SOMEONE HAD TOLD YOU.

OH WELL, AS THE BLESSED OSCAR PUT IT: "THERE IS ONLY ONE THING IN THE WORLD WORSE THAN BEING TALKED ABOUT..."

JUDGMENT NIGHT

THEY'RE HAVING SOMETHING CALLED SEX, HOOVER.

AND APPARENTLY ENJOYING IT IMMENSELY, AS I MYSELF USED TO BEFORE A CERTAIN FUCKING MORON ARRANGED TO HAVE ME *ANALLY RAPED.*

MR. STARR, I'VE *SAID* I'M SORRY--

WHICH EASES THE AGONY OF PASSING A BLOODY STOOL NO END.

YOU KNOW, IF WE DO END UP HAVING TO TERMINATE ANYONE, I CAN THINK OF WORSE PLACES TO DO IT...

eh?

LOOK AROUND YOU.

CAN YOU REALLY SEE ANY OF THESE PEOPLE CALLING THE POLICE?

"IT WAS TERRIBLE, OFFICER. THERE I WAS, JAMMING A SYRINGE FULL OF HEROIN INTO MY EYEBALL WHILE FELLATING A BILLY-GOAT, WHEN THESE MEN BURST IN AND STARTED *SHOOTING* PEOPLE.

"AREN'T WE EVEN SAFE AT OUR OWN ORGIES ANYMORE?"

I DON'T KNOW IF I CAN HANDLE MORE KILLING, NOT AFTER THAT GUY GALLICO...

GOD, HOOVER, YOU REALLY ARE USELESS, AREN'T YOU? GO AND WAIT WITH FEATHERSTONE AT THE TRANSPORT.

THE REST OF YOU SPREAD OUT. *FIND JESSE CUSTER.*

209

AYE, WELL, IT'S DIFFERENT STROKES FOR DIFFERENT FOLKS, ISN'T IT? WE CAN FIT IN HERE, AS SOON AS WE FIND SOME COMMON GROUND...

OH, FACE FACTS, BOB!

NOBODY *WANTS* TO TALK TO US. WE'RE THE SAD BASTARDS YOU SEE AT EVERY PARTY, STUCK IN THE CORNER ALL BY THEMSELVES...

IT'S ALL THAT BLOODY JESUS DeSADE'S FAULT! WE DELIVERED THE SMACK FOR HIM, AN' ALL WE GET FOR IT'S THE COLD FOOKIN' SHOULDER!

IT'S JUST NOT FAIR, FREDDY!

AW, SORRY, MATE--

THERE'S NO FOOKIN' JUSTICE!

HERE...DON'T I *KNOW* THAT FUCKIN' BRIT ACCENT...?

I HAVEN'T SEEN LORD JESUS--BUT LOOK, I'VE GOT AN EXHIBITION COMING UP AT *MOMA,* AND BIG SADIE'S AGREED TO POSE FOR MY *"GAZE INTO THE ABYSS"* PIECE!

WOULD YOU LIKE TO POSE WITH HER? I CAN JUST SEE YOU, GAZING INTO--

210

AAH--

YEEEOW!

I WANT CUSTER. I KNOW YOU KNOW HIM.

YOU WILL TELL ME WHERE HE IS OR I WILL BLOW YOUR FACE OFF THE FRONT OF YOUR SKULL.

WHERE IS JESSE CUSTER?!

FUCK YOU--

TULIP!

YOU KNOW THIS WOMAN? IN FIVE SECONDS' TIME SHE WILL HAVE NO FACE, UNLESS I AM TOLD WHERE TO FIND CUSTER. FOUR. THREE.

NO--DON'T-- HE'S JUST--

TWO.

IT'S ME!

I'M JESSE CUSTER.

GAWD DEMMIT.

ABOUT FUCKING TIME.

TAKE HIM. GATHER OUR DEAD.

KEEP A GUN ON THE WOMAN.

WE'RE LEAVING.

THE WOMAN IS IN THE OTHER VAN.

YOU CLEARLY CARE ABOUT HER, CUSTER. I WOULD HAZARD A GUESS THAT SHE BELONGS TO YOU.

I CAN TELL YOU RIGHT NOW THAT YOU WILL NEVER SEE HER AGAIN. YOUR ONLY CHANCE OF ENSURING HER SURVIVAL, HOWEVER, IS TO DO *EXACTLY* WHAT I TELL YOU:

BECAUSE ONE WORD FROM ME INTO THIS RADIO, AND MY MEN WILL LEAVE HER DEAD IN A DITCH.

FOR FOOK'S SAKE! STOP! AAAAAHH!

CAN'T BELIEVE I'M DOIN' NINETY MILES AN HOUR AN' THERE'S A FAT GUY ON THE CAR WITH HIS DICK OUT...

PRETENDIN' TO BE *ME*?

THE GUY WAS GOING TO SHOOT ME. I SUPPOSE HE THOUGHT IT WAS THE ONLY WAY... AND ONCE THEY GOT US APART IT WAS TOO LATE TO SAY DIFFERENT.

JESSE?

WHERE *WERE* YOU?

...NOT WHERE I SHOULDA BEEN, I GUESS.

SAMSON UNIT, THIS IS GABRIEL SIX. WE HAVE YOU IN SIGHT. PLEASE TRANSMIT CODE FOR SAFE PASSAGE, OVER.

TOP CODE *ALMIGHTY*, GABRIEL SIX. EXPECT ONE MOST BLESSED, ONE HEATHEN, OUTBOUND FOR MASADA, OVER.

ROGER THAT, SAMSON. SIX OUT.

YOU'D BETTER GET USED TO THE IDEA, REVEREND.

YOUR LIFE HAS CHANGED FOREVER.

MIRACLE MAN

HOW WAS YOUR TIME IN SAN FRANCISCO, HERR STARR?

A PAIN IN THE ARSE, BUT AT LEAST I GOT WHAT I WENT THERE FOR. ANY WORD FROM D'ARONIQUE?

THE ALLFATHER IS WAITING FOR YOUR REPORT, BUT TO THE BEST OF MY KNOWLEDGE HE HASN'T LEFT Le SAINT-MARIE.

GOOD. THE LAST THING I NEED NOW IS HIM POKING AROUND.

ON THAT SUBJECT, HERR STARR:

AS YOU KNOW, VERY FEW OF THE GRAIL PERSONNEL HERE ARE WITH US. I'VE TAKEN THE PRECAUTION OF CREWING YOUR JEEP WITH THREE OF THEM, SO YOU CAN TALK FREELY...

BUT OTHERWISE WATCH MY MOUTH.

OKAY, I'LL CALL D'ARONIQUE TOMORROW. I DON'T KNOW WHAT HE WANTS WITH CUSTER, BUT I'D RATHER HE FOUND OUT WE'RE HOLDING THE GOOD REVEREND LATER RATHER THAN SOONER.

AND ONE LAST THING, SIR. THE CALL YOU TOLD US TO EXPECT FROM FEATHERSTONE HAS NOT COME THROUGH.

THEN FIND OUT WHY THE FUCK NOT. FEATHERSTONE IS HOLDING CUSTER'S WOMAN, WHICH IS THE ONLY HOLD WE HAVE OVER HIM.

REPORT TO ME AT OH-ONE HUNDRED.

GO, DRIVER.

A WORD OF EXPLANATION, REVEREND.

ABOUT GAWD DEMN TIME...

235

I DON'T BELIEVE THIS--!

EH?

THE POINT IS THAT WHEN CIVILIZATION FALLS APART--AND IT WILL--THE GRAIL CAN PRODUCE A MORTAL MAN WHOSE ANCESTOR WAS BORN OF HEAVEN. A RELIGIOUS ALTERNATIVE TO FAILED POLITICIANS. A GOD-KING.

IT DOESN'T MATTER *WHO* WE PUT FORWARD. WE'VE GOT SO MANY OLD SCROLLS AND BULLSHIT DOCUMENTATION LYING AROUND, WE COULD PROVE CONCLUSIVELY THAT NEWT FUCKING GINGRICH IS THE SON OF GOD...

SUIT YOURSELF. I'M NOT EVEN SURE I DO.

THE LATEST PRODUCT OF THE BLOODLINE HAS TURNED OUT LESS THAN PERFECTLY. IF WE ARE TO HOLD SWAY AFTER THE COMING ARMAGEDDON, WE MUST GIVE THE MASSES A SAVIOR THEY CAN BELIEVE IN.

A SAVIOR WHO SPEAKS WITH A VOICE THAT MUST BE OBEYED WOULD BE IDEAL. IT'S YOU, REVEREND CUSTER.

I WANT YOU TO BE THE NEW MESSIAH.

AW, FUCKIN' GREAT!

...I MEAN BLESSED ARE THE MEEK.

IT *HAS* TO BE BULLSHIT...

'CEPT I USED THE WORD ON 'EM. TRUE OR NOT, THEY BELIEVE IT.

AN' IF GOD CAN GO MISSIN' FROM HEAVEN, WHY CAN'T HIS SON FAKE THE CRUCIFIXION? ONCE IT *LOOKS* LIKE HE'S DONE IT, THE HUMAN RACE CAN CONSIDER ITSELF REDEEMED. HE WOULDN'T HAVE TO DO IT FOR REAL.

BUT ENOUGH THEOLOGY. I'M GETTIN' A HANKERIN' TO PUNCH SOME MOTHERFUCKER'S TEETH OUT.

WHAT, THESE TWO?

HUH? NO, THEY'RE JUST GOOFS. GET A LOCATION ON THIS MASADA OUT'VE 'EM AN' THEN FIND SOME WAY TO KEEP 'EM FROM CALLIN' STARR

'CAUSE ONCE HE FINDS OUT CASS AIN'T ME, HE'S GONNA BE PLENTY PISSED.

YOU DON'T MEAN WE HAVE TO... GET RID OF THEM, DO YOU?

JESUS NO, HONEY. I AIN'T ABOUT TO START KILLIN' DEFENSELESS FOLKS, EVEN ASSHOLES LIKE HOOVER AN' FEATHERSTONE.

NO, IT'S THIS *STARR* SON OF A BITCH I WANT WORDS WITH. I DON'T LIKE THE GRAIL OR HIS GODDAMN CONSPIRACY INSIDE OF IT, AN' I SURE AS HELL DON'T LIKE HIS PLANS FOR WHERE I FIGURE IN IT, EITHER...

GONNA RESCUE CASS AN' THEN KICK THAT BASTARD'S ASS SO HARD HE'S GOTTA GO TO THE MOON TO SHIT.

OKAY, YOU CRAZY KIDS:

ROAD TRIP.

QUITE SOME PLACE YOU GOT HERE...

MM. THE EARLY FATHERS OF THE GRAIL BUILT MASADA WHEN THEY FLED HERE FROM ISRAEL.

WHY *MASADA?*

I THINK BECAUSE OF WHAT THE NAME SIGNIFIED FOR THEM: A SACRIFICE THAT INSPIRED AN UNDYING LEGEND. THEY HAD MADE A LOT OF SACRIFICES BY THEN.

YEAH, WHAT WERE THEY FLEEIN' FROM, EXACTLY?

PERSECUTION. JUST IN GENERAL, I THINK, NOT SPECIFIC TO THEM. THE HOLY LAND WAS NO MORE STABLE FOURTEEN HUNDRED YEARS AGO THAN IT IS TODAY.

...AH WAS GONNA SAY, IT'S KINDA WEIRD A KRAUT FELLA LIKE YERSELF TIED UP IN ALLA THIS JEWISH STUFF...

ONE, IT'S MORE CHRISTIAN THAN JEWISH. TWO, I HAVE NEVER BEEN A RACIST. AND THREE, MY NATIONALITY CEASED TO MEAN ANYTHING THE INSTANT I JOINED THE GRAIL.

I AM A SOLDIER, REVEREND. AND I FIGHT IN THE ONLY WAR THAT MATTERS.

YEAH?

THE WAR FOR ETERNITY.

THE WAR THAT DECIDES THE FATE OF THE WORLD: AND WHETHER IT WILL BE RULED BY THE FORCES OF ORDER, OR DESTROYED BY THE FORCES OF CHAOS. THE WAR FOR *CONTROL.*

THE SHEEP NEED THEIR SHEPHERD.

BUT WHY D'YOU WANT TO CONTROL PEOPLE...?

BECAUSE THEY CAN NO MORE CONTROL THEIR OWN DESTINIES THAN THE FLOCK CAN PROTECT ITSELF FROM THE WOLF-PACK. AND WHEN DESTINY FALLS VICTIM TO CHAOS, IT IS RENDERED POINTLESS.

THE GRAIL KNOWS WHAT IS BEST FOR PEOPLE, REVEREND. WE ARE LIKE GOD IN THAT RESPECT.

NOW: I DON'T KNOW EXACTLY WHAT YOU'VE BEEN DOING SINCE THAT FIRESTORM OBLITERATED YOUR CONGREGATION, BUT I AM AWARE OF THIS POWER THAT YOU HAVE.

I WOULD LIKE TO SEE IT DEMONSTRATED.

uh--

PAUL? COME AND MEET REVEREND CUSTER.

BONJOUR... REVEREND... CUSTER...

PAUL IS NINETY-FOUR. HE HAS WORKED HERE IN THE GARDENS OF MASADA ALL HIS LIFE. HE HAS BEEN LAME FOR THIRTY YEARS.

I WANT YOU TO CURE HIM.

WHAT?

HEAL HIM WITH YOUR VOICE. COMMAND HIM TO CAST ASIDE HIS CRUTCHES AND WALK WITHOUT THEM.

I WOULD REMIND YOU WE STILL HAVE YOUR WOMAN...

243

ABOUT TIME, FEATHERSTONE. IS THE GIRL SECURE?

WHAT? HOW COULD YOU--

WHAT DO YOU MEAN, WE HAVEN'T GOT HIM?

NO. NO, THAT'S IMPOSSIBLE. INSANE. HOW COULD THAT BE?

HE...HE DID? YES, BUT--

NO, I'LL CALL YOU. GET YOUR PEOPLE SEARCHING FOR THIS OTHER INDIVIDUAL. AND STAND BY.

YES, SIR.

WHERE'S... 'CUSTER'...?

WE GAVE HIM A ROOM AS YOU INSTRUCTED, WHY?

I NEED...TO CHECK SOMETHING.

HAVE HIM BROUGHT TO CELL NINETY-NINE. DETAIL THOSE THREE GUARDS TO DO IT.

AND ON YOUR WAY THERE, DROP BY THE ARMORY AND PICK ME UP A MACHINE GUN.

246

YOU DON'T REALLY THINK THAT OF ME, DO YOU, BABY? LET'S NOT--uh--SPOIL THE MOOD...

HANDS OFF.

TULIP, YOU SEEN WHAT THESE GRAIL BOYS ARE LIKE. THEY GOT GUNS, THEY GOT CONNECTIONS --HELL, IT SOUNDS LIKE THEY GOT A WHOLE GODDAMN ARMY OF THEIR OWN, AN' WE'LL BE GOIN' AFTER THEM ON THEIR HOME GROUND...

I SAW *EXACTLY* WHAT THEY'RE LIKE, BECAUSE I HAD TO SHOOT IT OUT WITH THEM SINGLE-HANDED WHILE YOU WERE OFF GOD KNOWS WHERE! FUCKING *CASSIDY* HAD TO RESCUE ME!

IF THAT'S AN EXAMPLE OF YOUR PROTECTION, YOU KNOW WHAT YOU CAN DO WITH IT...

OKAY, I FUCKED UP! THAT'S WHY I'M *TWICE* AS DETERMINED NOT TO PUT YOU IN THE SAME KINDA TROUBLE AGAIN!

LOOK, THERE'S SOMETHING YOU JUST DON'T SEEM TO UNDERSTAND ABOUT WOMEN: WE CAN TAKE CARE OF OUR-SELVES. WE WANT TO. WE *LIKE THE IDEA*...

THAT'S SO TRUE, HOW WAS IT CASS HAD TO RESCUE YOU?

WELL, HOW COME *YOU* WEREN'T THERE TO?

BUT IF YOU CAN TAKE CARE OF YOURSELF, WHY WOULD I--

AW FUCK, ALL WE'RE DOIN' IS GOIN' ROUND IN GODDAMN CIRCLES...!

SEEMS TO ME THERE'S SOMETHIN' YOU DON'T KNOW ABOUT MEN, AN' THAT'S THAT WE CAN'T HELP THIS SHIT.

I MEAN, I DUNNO IF IT'S GENETIC OR IF IT'S TO DO WITH WHAT WE GET TAUGHT, OR IF IT'S JUST 'CAUSE IT'S EXPECTED OF US--BUT IT'S WHAT WE *DO*, OKAY?

'CAUSE TO HELP A GIRL WHEN SHE'S IN TROUBLE, OR STOP HER GETTIN' INTO TROUBLE, IS JUST THE RIGHT GODDAMNED THING TO DO.

AN' I *KNOW* YOU'RE AS SMART AS ME, AN' AS CAPABLE, AN' MY EQUAL AT JUST ABOUT EVERYTHING--I KNOW YOU'RE *EMPOWERED*, OR WHATEVER THE HELL YOU CALL IT--BUT I SWEAR, I EVEN THINK OF A SINGLE HAIR ON YOUR HEAD GETTIN' HARMED AN' ALL THAT BULLSHIT GOES RIGHT OUT THE FUCKIN' WINDOW...

WHERE DID YOU LEARN STUFF LIKE "EMPOWERED"..?

NEEDED SOME-THIN' TO BRIGHTEN UP MY HANGOVERS BACK IN ANNVILLE, SO I HIT THE TOWN LIBRARY. WORKED MY WAY FROM A TO Z.

YOU READ THE *WHOLE* LIBRARY?

HAD FIVE YEARS.

FOUND *FEMINIST THEORY* UNDER F, BELIEVE IT OR NOT. HAD ME QUITE A TIME. DEFINITELY PREFER GERMAINE GREER OVER THE DWORKIN WOMAN.

YOU GET ME THAT CIGARETTE NOW?

YEAH, I'LL DEMEAN MYSELF AND FETCH YOU YOUR DAMN CIGARETTE...

YOU REMEMBER ANGELVILLE?

WHAT DO YOU THINK?

I BEGGED FOR YOUR LIFE THAT DAY, BABY. I BEGGED JODY TO LET YOU GO IN THE VAN, AN' THEN I DID THE SAME THING NEXT MORNIN' WITH GRAN'MA.

I SAID I'D DO JUST ABOUT ANYTHING THEY WANTED IF THEY DIDN'T HURT YOU, AN' I MEANT IT. I'D A GONE BACK TO THE MINISTRY, OR GIVEN THAT OL' BITCH A GRAND-SON--HELL, I WOULDA TURNED MY BACK ON *YOU* IF IT MEANT YOU COULD WALK OUTTA THERE UNHARMED...

YOU IMAGINE ANY OTHER CIRCUMSTANCE IN THE WHOLE GODDAMN WORLD-- *EVER*--WHERE I WOULD BEG *ANYONE* FOR ANYTHING?

heh. NO, I CAN'T SEE IT, SOMEHOW.

...WHAT'S YOUR POINT?

MY POINT IS, THERE'S ONLY ONE THING IN THIS LIFE THAT SCARES ME, AN' THAT'S THE THOUGHT OF YOU EVER GETTIN' HURT AGAIN.

CAN'T YOU SEE WHAT IT'LL DO TO ME, YOU COMIN' ALONG IN FRANCE WITH THESE FUCKS OUT TO GET US?

MM. WELL.

I GUESS YOU'LL HAVE TO LEARN TO LIVE WITH IT, REVEREND.

GO TO SLEEP.

...YOU GIRLS SURE ARE HARD ON THE BOYS THAT LOVE YOU.

DO NOT STOP.

NO SIR!

...AND RELOAD. CHECK HIM.

SIR...? HERR STARR?

I THINK HE'S STILL ALIVE.

THAT'S SOMETHING WE'LL HAVE TO WORK ON.

THIS IS CLEARLY NOT THE MAN WE WANTED, BUT BASED ON WHAT FEATHERSTONE TOLD ME, I THINK I CAN HAZARD A GUESS:

JESSE CUSTER IS COMING TO US.